W9-BVN-405

WITHDRAWN

SEATTLE WORLD SCHOOL LIBRARY

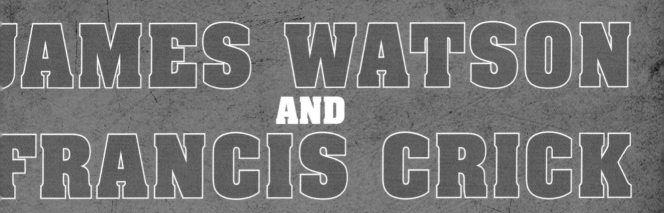

JAMES WATSON
AND
FRANCIS CRICK

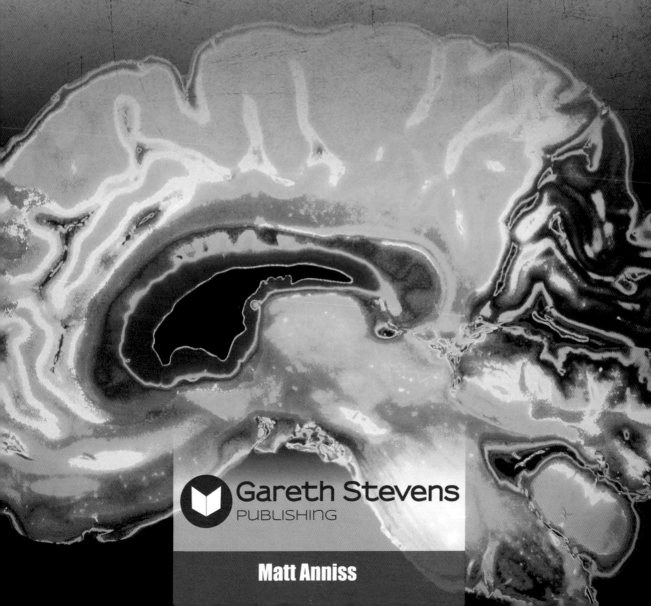

Gareth Stevens
PUBLISHING

Matt Anniss

Please visit our website, **www.garethstevens.com**. For a free color catalog of all our high-quality books, call toll free 1-800-542-2595 or fax 1-877-542-2596.

Library of Congress Cataloging-in-Publication Data

Anniss, Matt.
James Watson and Francis Crick / by Matt Anniss.
p. cm. -- (Dynamic duos of science)
Includes index.
ISBN 978-1-4824-1294-9 (pbk.)
ISBN 978-1-4824-1282-6 (6-pack)
ISBN 978-1-4824-1471-4 (library binding)
1. Watson, James D., -- 1928- -- Juvenile literature. 2. Crick, Francis, -- 1916-2004 -- Juvenile literature. 3. DNA -- Research -- Juvenile literature. I. Anniss, Matt. II. Title.
QP620.A56 2015
574.87--d23

First Edition

Published in 2015 by
Gareth Stevens Publishing
111 East 14th Street, Suite 349
New York, NY 10003

© Gareth Stevens Publishing

Produced by: Calcium, www.calciumcreative.co.uk
Designed by: Keith Williams
Edited by: Sarah Eason and Jennifer Sanderson
Picture research by: Rachel Blount

Photo credits: Cover: Shutterstock: Paul Fleet (background); Wikimedia Commons: Cold Spring Harbor Laboratory (left), Marc Lieberman (right); Inside: Dreamstime: Stefano Cavoretto 35, Dml5050 36, Elena Elisseeva 16, 30b, Sebastian Kaulitzki 20, Kwiktor 34, Molekuul 30t, Katie Nesling 1, 41, Leung Cho Pan 27, Photographerlondon 39, Marina Scurupii 44, Shotsstudio 29, Showface 38, Skypixel 9, Sofiaworld 21, Johannes Gerhardus Swanepoel 10, Wavebreakmedia Ltd 45; Flickr: Royal Institution 31, Science Museum, London 28; King's College, London: R Franklin and R Gosling 32; Library of Congress: Keystone View Co. 7; Shutterstock: Awe Inspiring Images 18, BlueRingMedia 33, Catwalker 37, Dirima 17, Dream designs 23, Paul Fleet 3, 5b, Bucchi Francesco 14, Sebastian Kaulitzki 13, Micimakin 43, Monkey Business Images 22, Panu Ruangjan 11; US National Library of Medicine: 15, 24; Wikimedia Commons: 25, Cold Spring Harbor Laboratory 5t, Daderot 12, Marc Lieberman 4, Magerius 6, Marjorie McCarty 19, National Archives and Records Administration 8, Russ London 42, Smithsonian Institution Archives 26.

All rights reserved. No part of this book may be reproduced in any form
without permission from the publisher, except by reviewer.

Printed in the United States of America

CPSIA compliance information: Batch #CS15GS: For further information contact Gareth Stevens, New York, New York at 1-800-542-2595.

Contents

CHAPTER 1

Scientific Geniuses

Throughout history, extraordinary scientists have made discoveries that have revolutionized our understanding of the world around us. In the eighteenth century, an Austrian monk named Gregor Mendel discovered that all living things pass on genes to their offspring. In the nineteenth century, Charles Darwin put forward the theory of evolution. Then, in the early twentieth century, scientists began to discover more about how genes make us who we are.

In 1953, James Watson and Francis Crick sent shockwaves around the world by announcing that they had figured out the riddle of deoxyribonucleic acid (DNA), a substance carried deep inside each of the many billions of tiny body cells in every living thing, from people to plants.

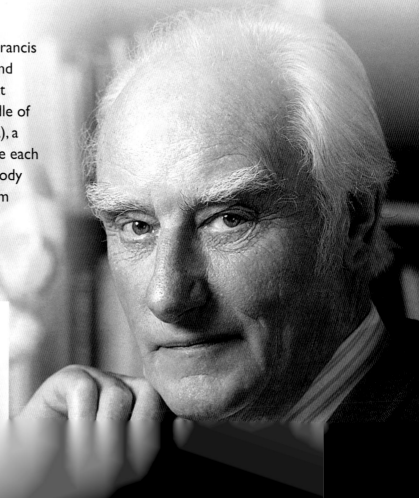

Francis Crick's contribution to science is so significant that a $1 million research center named after him will open in London, England, in 2015.

Changing History

Watson and Crick's discovery was so enormous that it changed the path of science forever. By unlocking the mystery of DNA, Watson and Crick had, in fact, discovered the secret of all life on Earth.

James Watson has received many awards and prizes for his pioneering DNA work, including the Liberty Medal, the Presidential Medal of Freedom, and the Benjamin Franklin Medal for Distinguished Achievement in the Sciences.

BEHIND THE SCIENCE

Gregor Mendel was the first scientist to discover the importance of genes. By carefully experimenting with pea plants over a seven-year period, he observed that plants inherit certain traits from their parents and grandparents, such as wrinkled seeds, large pods, or yellow coloring. Just like pea plants, humans pass on genes to their children and grandchildren—however, until Watson and Crick explained DNA, no one knew how the traits were passed on.

Worlds Apart

Although Watson and Crick would eventually become one of the most famous scientific partnerships the world has ever seen, it took an unlikely chain of events to bring the two scientists together. Watson and Crick were born years apart and on different continents. If their lives had taken different paths, they may never have met.

The Young Crick

Francis Harry Crick was born on June 8, 1916, in Northampton, England. Northampton is a small town famous for its shoemaking industry. Crick's father, Harry Crick, ran the family's shoe and boot factory. Crick had an ordinary childhood and attended good schools. After receiving a children's encyclopedia as a gift, he developed a great interest in science and told his mother he wanted to be a scientist when he grew up. By the age of 12, Crick was already conducting basic chemistry experiments in his Uncle Walter's shed.

The money from the Crick family's shoemaking business, which was based at a factory like this one in Northampton, England, helped pay for Crick to be educated at private schools.

Manufacturer COPYRIGHTED WASHINGTON, U.S.A. Publishers

Meadville, Pa., New York, N.Y., Chicago, Ill., London, England.

18453 In the Heart of the Great Shopping Center State St. Chicago, Ill.

When he was growing up in the 1930s, the bustling city of Chicago did not interest Watson. He preferred being in the countryside where he could study birds and animals.

The Young Watson

At the same time as young Crick was discovering science, on the other side of the Atlantic Ocean his future laboratory partner was just a baby. James Dewey Watson was born on April 6, 1928, in Chicago, Illinois. From a very young age, Watson had a great interest in the world around him and continually asked his parents questions about the creatures and objects he saw. He was fascinated by how organisms survived and functioned. Watson grew up believing that science could provide the answers to most of life's greatest questions.

IN THEIR OWN WORDS

Crick said:

"I wanted to know 'what is the world made of?' Because I asked so many questions, my parents bought me something called *Children's Encyclopedia*. That covered all subjects—history, books, and music as well as science."

The Fast-Talking Englishman

By the age of 14, Crick had excelled at his Northampton Grammar School and had earned a place at a private school in London. This was the stroke of fortune that established Crick's scientific career and place in history.

Crick got great grades in math, physics, and chemistry and, at 18 years old, was given a place to study physics at University College, London. In 1937, he graduated with a degree in physics.

Crick stayed on as a research student and was so successful that he was awarded the Carey Foster Research Prize in 1939, which is a great honor for young scientists.

London was a dangerous place during World War II. German planes dropped thousands of bombs onto the city and destroyed hundreds of important buildings, including Crick's laboratory.

8

With his physics background, studying human body cells was a sizeable challenge for Crick, but one that excited him enormously.

A Change of Plan

Crick was looking forward to a career in physics when World War II broke out. After a German bomb fell through the roof of his laboratory and destroyed his equipment, Crick decided to join the military.

He worked for the Admiralty, designing mines that were made to help resist a German invasion of Britain. When Crick left the military in 1947, he was uncertain about his future. He knew that he wanted to return to research, so he enrolled at the University of Cambridge, England. Crick had become disillusioned with physics and wanted a new challenge. In 1949, he got the break he was looking for—the chance to study human body cells at the university's Strangeways Laboratory.

IN THEIR OWN WORDS

Of his early science career, Crick said:

"By the time most scientists have reached age 30, they are trapped by their own expertise. I, on the other hand, knew nothing."

The Quiz Kid

Even as a child, it was clear that Watson was exceptionally intelligent. He was so gifted that he frequently complained of being bored in class, which did not make him popular with his classmates.

Watson became interested in science at an early age, largely through his father's bird-watching hobby. His dad, James Sr., would take Watson along on bird-watching trips, pointing out different types of bird when he spotted them. It was not long before young Jimmy, as his father called him, became fascinated with more than simply looking at birds: he wanted to find out everything he could about them, too. It soon became clear that young Watson thought like a scientist.

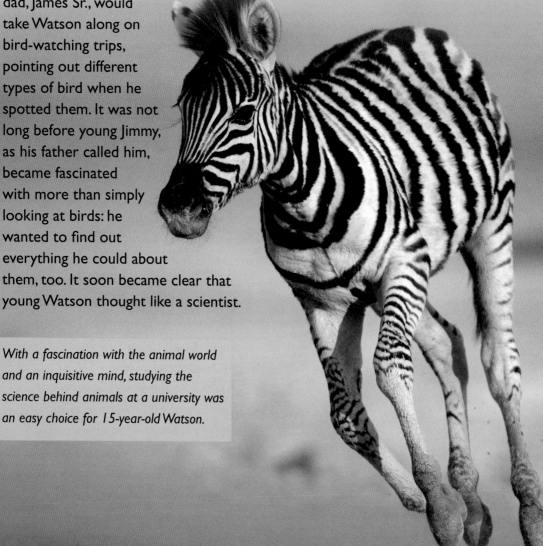

With a fascination with the animal world and an inquisitive mind, studying the science behind animals at a university was an easy choice for 15-year-old Watson.

Ornithology, the scientific name for the study of birds, was Watson's chosen specialist subject while studying zoology at the University of Chicago.

Child Genius

When he was 12, Watson was asked to appear on a local radio program in Chicago, a game show called *Quiz Kids*. The show featured preteens who answered tough questions that would puzzle many adults. Watson won a few episodes and enough prize money to buy a savings bond in the process.

As he grew older, Watson decided to go to college to pursue a career in science. He believed that he would have to wait until he was 18, like most other students, before he could enroll at college. However, local college president Robert Hutchins could see Watson's outstanding ability and decided otherwise. Hutchins offered Watson a place at the University of Chicago when he was just 15 years old. Watson took the place and enrolled in a zoology course. His journey to scientific superstardom had just begun.

BEHIND THE SCIENCE

Zoology is the study of the animal kingdom, including mammals, reptiles, birds, and fish. Zoologists study animal anatomy, behavior, evolution, and classification.

A Twist of Fate

In 1946, Watson read a book that would change his life forever. The book was *What Is Life?* by Erwin Schrödinger, a scientist best known for his work in physics. In his groundbreaking book, Schrödinger argued that genes were the most important area of biology. He stated that scientists should strive to discover all they could about genes, believing this would lead to further breakthroughs in the understanding of not only how the human body works, but also how human evolution unfolded over millions of years.

Schrödinger's book inspired Watson. He wanted to work in the field of genetics, which is the study of genes. To further his career in genetics, Watson knew he needed to find out more about molecular biology, the study of cells. He found work as a researcher at Indiana University, under the supervision of future Nobel Prize winner Salvador Luria.

Until Schrödinger's interest in DNA, it was believed to be an unimportant cell feature.

$$i\hbar\,\dot{\psi} = H\psi$$

Watson's mentor, Salvador Luria, believed that bacteriophages, one of the simplest lifeforms on the planet, might help him understand how living things reproduce exact copies of their body cells.

A Common Interest

Meanwhile, across the Atlantic, Watson's future laboratory partner, Crick, had also become a fan of Schrödinger's book. Crick later praised the book in his autobiography, saying that Schrödinger "made it seem that great things were just around the corner." In the future, Schrödinger's book would become one of the common interests that drew Watson and Crick together.

BEHIND THE SCIENCE

During his work with Salvador Luria, Watson studied bacteriophages. These are simple lifeforms with very few cells, usually viruses. Luria believed that they might hold the key to unlocking the secrets of genetics.

CHAPTER 2

On the Path of Discovery

In 1950, Salvador Luria helped Watson to move to Copenhagen, Denmark, where he planned to continue his studies in molecular biology. While in Copenhagen, Watson was sent to a science conference in Naples, Italy, in 1951.

In Naples, Watson attended a talk by an English scientist named Maurice Wilkins, who specialized in a process called X-ray diffraction. In the 1950s, this was a cutting-edge research technique. It involved creating accurate images of molecules on photographic paper by firing X-rays at the molecules. The diffraction patterns that emerged were then studied.

Studying chemistry in the beautiful city of Copenhagen was one of the most challenging times of Watson's career because he struggled to understand the broken English used by his Danish boss.

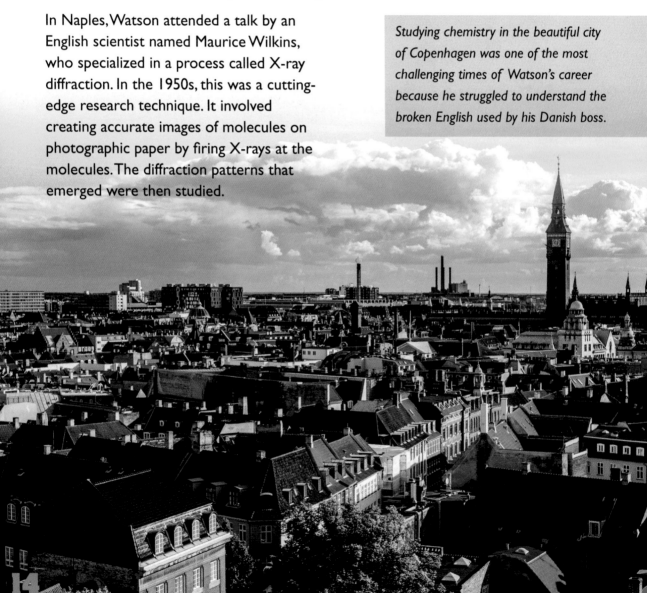

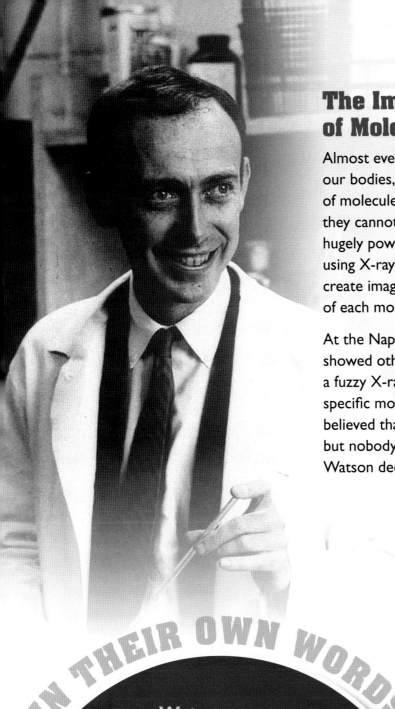

The Importance of Molecules

Almost everything around us, including our bodies, is made up of many billions of molecules. Molecules are so small that they cannot be seen without the aid of hugely powerful microscopes. However, using X-ray diffraction, it is possible to create images that show the structure of each molecule.

At the Naples conference in 1951, Wilkins showed other scientists, including Watson, a fuzzy X-ray diffraction image of one specific molecule: DNA. Many scientists believed that genes were made of DNA, but nobody knew how. There and then, Watson decided to solve the riddle.

Watson, shown here as an enthusiastic young scientist, was just 23 years old when he became obsessed with genetics, molecular biology, and DNA.

IN THEIR OWN WORDS

Watson was so inspired by Wilkins's talk, he said:

"After Maurice's talk, I knew that genes could crystallize. Therefore, DNA must have a structure that could be solved in a straightforward way."

A Meeting of Minds

Excited by the possibility of unlocking the secrets of DNA, Watson decided his future lay not in Denmark but in Cambridge, England. At the University of Cambridge, the inventor of the X-ray diffraction technique, Sir Lawrence Bragg, had established a new research center known as the Cavendish Laboratory.

The Cavendish Laboratory specialized in using X-ray diffraction techniques to study the structures of proteins, which are molecules made up of small units called amino acids. Proteins are found in every human body cell, so Watson believed that the study of them would play a major part in solving the DNA puzzle. He persuaded Bragg to take him on at the Cavendish Laboratory.

The models below show the molecular structure of amino acids. They are the tiny building blocks of all proteins, not just in humans but also in other living creatures such as animals. Amino acids become protein molecules when a large number connect to each other in a long chain. There are many different types of protein molecules, each made up of a slightly different combination of the 500 amino acids currently known to scientists. People get some of the 20 essential amino acids that the body needs from food.

Watson and Crick Meet

Watson arrived in Cambridge in October 1951 and immediately began working with Bragg's colleague, Max Perutz. Perutz introduced Watson to another member of the Cavendish Laboratory research team, a 35-year-old scientist named Francis Crick.

Watson and Crick liked each other immediately. They did not work together to begin with, but it would be only a matter of time before they joined forces to pursue their shared goal—discovering the secrets of DNA and, with it, the secret of all life on Earth.

When we exercise, we use proteins to fire the chemical processes that turn stored food into energy. By exercising, we also strengthen our muscles and bones, a process that also requires protein. Protein is essential for human health.

BEHIND THE SCIENCE

Proteins serve many purposes in the human body. Some are found in muscles, others are used to help people grow, and some strengthen bones. Many proteins found in body cells help kick-start important chemical reactions, such as the production of new blood cells.

The Odd Couple

In many ways, Watson and Crick were an unlikely pairing. However, it was not long before they struck up a strong friendship and, within a few months, began working together.

Watson, the Outsider

When he arrived in Cambridge, Watson stood out, not because of his strong accent—still a rarity in England at the time—but because he had very short hair and dressed casually, unlike his peers.

Watson had very strong opinions, often clashed with people, and was thought of by the more reserved English scientists as bold. Despite his years of experience as a leading science student and researcher, Watson was still just 23 years old.

DNA Double Helix 1953
"The secret of life"
For decades the Eagle was the local
pub for scientists from the nearby
Cavendish Laboratory.
It was here on February 28th 1953 that
Francis Crick and James Watson first
announced their discovery of how
DNA carries genetic information.
Unveiled by James Watson
25th April 2003

A special commemorative plaque now sits on the wall outside Watson and Crick's favorite meeting place, a pub called The Eagle.

Although Watson and Crick found fame by discovering the structure of DNA, the molecule's importance was first understood by a group of American scientists including Maclyn McCarty, who is here seen meeting the pair in the late 1950s.

Crick, the Popular Scientist

Crick was known around the university for being loud and opinionated, but was generally well liked. He took every opportunity to take coworkers to the local pub, The Eagle, where he would tell stories and argue his scientific theories.

A Partnership

In Watson, Crick found a great companion. The pair soon discovered that they agreed on many subjects and enjoyed arguing about others. They complemented each other, too. While Watson had great experience in biology, Crick had a better knowledge of physics. Together, they would form an awesome scientific partnership.

IN THEIR OWN WORDS

Watson and Crick got along so well, Watson said:

"From my first day in the lab I knew I would not leave Cambridge for a long time. Departing would be idiocy, because I had immediately discovered the fun of talking to Francis Crick."

CHAPTER 3

The Search for the Secret of Life

Watson and Crick became inseparable. They spent much of their time talking about areas of science that interested them when they should have been working!

Soon, the two scientists realized that they had a shared interest in discovering the structure and purpose of DNA. During the 1950s, this was seen as one of the greatest prizes in science, because it would, in turn, unlock many of the secrets of life on Earth. There were already many scientists around the world trying to find answers to the mystery of DNA. Watson and Crick decided to join the race.

Watson and Crick's obsession with DNA was fueled by the recent discovery that DNA molecules are the building blocks of every single part of the human body, including the nerve endings pictured below.

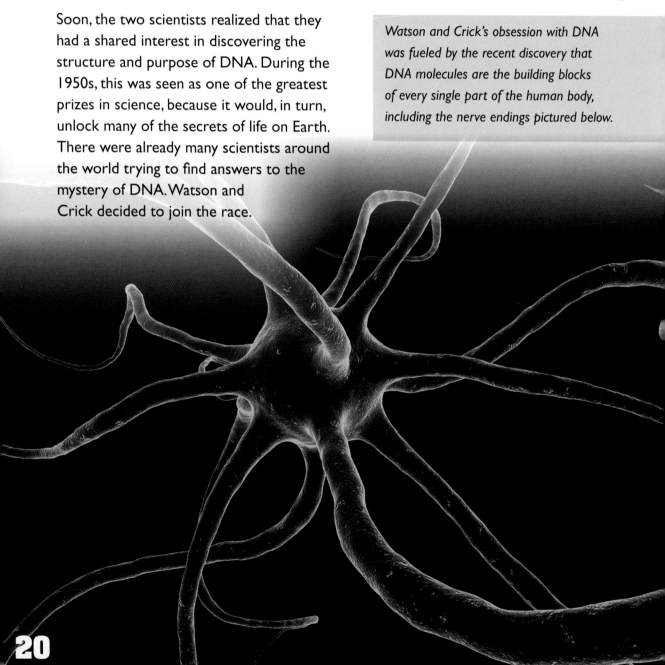

Watson and Crick made many different models, such as this one, before they finally figured out the correct molecular structure of DNA.

The First DNA Model

Using their existing knowledge and the research work of Wilkins and his team, Watson and Crick decided to make a three-dimensional model of what they believed the DNA molecule might look like. They used wires and small plastic balls to construct the model, but it was spectacularly wrong.

When Bragg found out about Watson and Crick's work, he told the two scientists to return to their studies of proteins and viruses. Watson and Crick did as they were told, but the two scientists also continued their DNA research in secret.

BEHIND THE SCIENCE

Watson and Crick made models of what they believed DNA looked like because, at the time, microscopes were not powerful enough to see inside body cells. That is because each DNA molecule is around 1,000 times too small for the human eye to see.

What Is DNA?

Today, we know that DNA is the basis of life itself. It is found in almost every cell in every living thing on the planet. There are trillions of cells in each person's body, and at the center of each of most cells is a DNA molecule.

At the time that Watson and Crick began working together, scientists' understanding of DNA was limited. Watson and Crick knew that DNA has four chemical bases: adenine, thymine, guanine, and cytosine. This was thanks to the work of US scientist Erwin Chagraff, who, in 1950, had studied the chemicals in great detail. By 1952, Chagraff had proved that the same four chemicals were found in the DNA of every bird, animal, fish, and reptile on Earth, as well as in simpler lifeforms such as viruses. If DNA was fundamentally the same across all life forms, it must be fundamental to life itself.

DNA is a little like a tiny hard drive inside each of our body cells. Just as a hard drive contains all the information to operate a computer, DNA stores all the "data" our body needs to survive, from the color of our eyes and hair to how we behave.

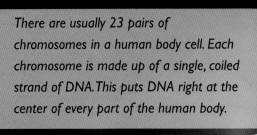

There are usually 23 pairs of chromosomes in a human body cell. Each chromosome is made up of a single, coiled strand of DNA. This puts DNA right at the center of every part of the human body.

DNA and Genetics

Scientists also knew that DNA played some part in the process of passing on characteristics from one generation to the next. They had already figured out that these characteristics are contained within long, thin substances called chromosomes, each of which contains thousands of genes. There are 46 chromosomes in each human cell. Scientists knew that chromosomes were made of DNA, but they did not know why. They also did not understand how DNA worked, how the various chemicals were arranged within the molecule, and how these chemicals interacted with each other. This was the puzzle that Watson and Crick were trying to solve.

IN THEIR OWN WORDS

Crick said:

"Almost every cell in our bodies has a complete set of genes within it, and this chemical program directs how each cell grows and interacts with its neighbors."

23

The Importance of X-Rays

Watson and Crick continued to build models of what they thought the structure of the DNA molecule might look like. In truth, they were struggling, and the model they first proposed was a failure.

One scientist who was particularly critical of their first model was Rosalind Franklin, a researcher who specialized in X-ray diffraction. She worked alongside Wilkins, the scientist whose talk in Naples had convinced Watson to devote his life to unlocking the secrets of DNA.

Franklin and Wilkins did not get along. She was a brilliant scientist and arguably a better X-ray crystallographer than her boss, Wilkins. She frequently argued with him and even accused him of stealing her groundbreaking ideas on several occasions.

Some scientists believe that it was actually Franklin who first discovered the exact structure of DNA, but Watson and Crick were credited with the find because they published their discovery first. Franklin's in-depth article on DNA appeared in Nature *a few months after Watson and Crick's in 1953.*

A Man's World

Franklin had created the clearest X-ray diffraction images of DNA molecules so far. The images were not particularly clear, but they were good enough to suggest new lines of research. If Watson and Crick were going to solve the DNA riddle, they would need the clues provided by Franklin and Wilkins's X-ray diffraction images. Wilkins was happy to exchange ideas with Watson and even shared the clearest X-ray diffraction images with the young American. Franklin, however, was not so eager because she wanted to figure out the structure of DNA herself and saw Watson and Crick as serious rivals.

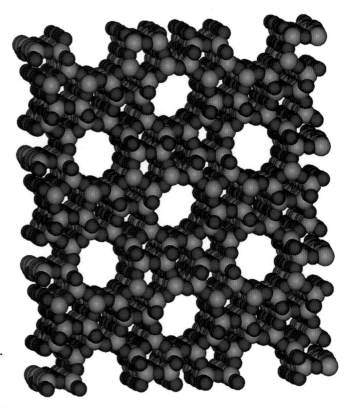

X-ray crystallography was first used to create images of the molecular structure of naturally occurring minerals. It was using this method that scientists first created detailed images, such as the one above, which shows the structure of the mineral zeolite.

BEHIND THE SCIENCE

X-ray crystallography is a scientific method of measuring atoms and molecules using invisible waves of energy called X-rays. The X-rays are fired at molecules from different angles using a machine called a goniometer. By measuring the patterns created by the reflections of the X-rays, scientists can figure out accurate models of the molecules.

The Alpha Helix

Across the Atlantic Ocean in the United States, scientist Linus Pauling was hard at work trying to figure out the exact structure of DNA. Based at the California Institute of Technology, Pauling was one of the country's brightest scientific minds.

Pauling had previously found fame by figuring out the nature of the chemical bonds between atoms and electrons, tiny particles of energy that are the basis of the entire universe. By 1949, he had turned his attention to molecular biology. It wasn't long before he would make his mark.

In 1951, Pauling announced to the world that he had figured out what he believed was the correct structure of all protein molecules. His research, which had taken him a number of years, suggested that the molecules had a unique shape, which had not been seen in science before. They were, he said, helical in shape, meaning that they looked like a coiled spring.

Pauling explained the significance of his "alpha helix" structure by likening it to a rope, in which individual strands of thread are interwoven to create a single, stronger object.

Protein Molecules and DNA

Protein molecules are extremely important because they do many different jobs within the body. Some, called enzymes, control chemical reactions, while others help muscles move. Some proteins provide body cells with a structure and play a role in helping our bodies fight against illness. The discovery of the alpha helix was a huge step forward for molecular biology: Pauling had proved that molecules could have a helical structure, in which long chains of acids and other chemicals were twisted into coil-like shapes. Scientists were inching closer to the discovery of the structure of DNA—the question was, who would win the race?

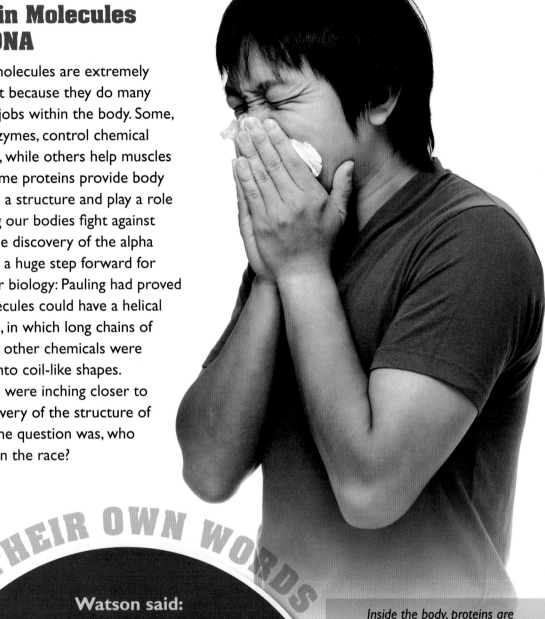

IN THEIR OWN WORDS

Watson said:

"A potential key to the secret of life was impossible to push out of my mind. It was certainly better to imagine myself becoming famous than maturing into a stifled academic who never risked a thought."

Inside the body, proteins are used to build and strengthen the immune system. This is the process the body uses to fight diseases and illnesses such as the common cold.

CHAPTER 4

The Race to Define DNA

When Watson and Crick began working in secret on a new model of the structure of DNA, they knew they would have to work quickly. The race to solve one of science's most puzzling problems was speeding up, and the finishing line was in sight.

Watson and Crick knew that their local rival, Franklin, was determined to beat them to the prize. Meanwhile in the United States, Pauling was working on a model based around the alpha helix he had seen in proteins. He believed DNA would have a helical structure, but he had still not figured out the details.

This is one of the few remaining fragments of the original aluminum model of the DNA molecule made by Watson and Crick in 1953. When complete, the model was several feet high.

Even today, more than 60 years after Watson and Crick's DNA discovery, scientists are still learning about the DNA molecule.

Figuring Out a Big Problem

All four scientists and Franklin's colleague, Wilkins, were wrestling with the same problem. They knew that DNA was made up of adenine, thymine, guanine, and cytosine as well as sugar and phosphate (another chemical found inside human cells in tiny quantities). However, they did not know how these components were arranged inside the DNA molecule itself. Figuring out the exact arrangement of the elements within the DNA structure would unlock even bigger secrets, such as how a person's body cells can make exact copies of themselves.

BEHIND THE SCIENCE

In 1952, US scientists **Alfred Hershey** and **Martha Chase** conducted an experiment with a virus using a kitchen blender. By separating out the different elements of the cell using the blender, they conclusively proved that it was **DNA** that carried the genetic information that allowed cells—and by extension human beings—to reproduce.

False Starts

In February 1953, Pauling published a report proposing a structure for DNA. It was based around the helical structure he had first discovered in proteins. Instead of proposing a single helix, like the alpha helix, Pauling's report featured three helixes wrapped around each other. He called this the "triple helix."

Watson and Crick were devastated by the publication. They believed that they were close to a breakthrough but had not solved many of the problems Pauling appeared to have overcome. Pauling had arranged the phosphates on the inside of the helixes, with the chemical bases on the outside. At first glance, it seemed that Pauling had the DNA structure absolutely right.

Before the discovery of the true structure of DNA, many scientists, including Pauling, Watson, and Crick, believed that the molecule was a "triple helix," as shown above right and below. Amazingly, they were all wrong.

Bragg played a key role in the discovery of the structure of DNA. Not only was he Watson and Crick's boss at the Cavendish Laboratory in Cambridge, he also invented the system of X-ray diffraction used by Wilkins and Franklin.

A Big Break

Fortunately for Watson and Crick, Pauling had made some serious mistakes. He had gotten his calculations wrong, and the phosphates were in the wrong place. They could not tie the triple helix together, and therefore every molecule would collapse in on itself. The discovery was a huge blow to Pauling, but it gave Watson and Crick an enormous boost. Now they had more time to develop their model. With the blessing of their boss, Bragg, they openly returned to work on their model of DNA.

IN THEIR OWN WORDS

About where the phosphates should be in the model, Crick said:

"I said to James one evening: 'Why not build DNA models with the phosphates on the outside?' He said 'That would be too easy.' So I said, 'Why not try it?'"

31

The Eureka Moment

Shortly after realizing that Pauling's triple helix model was wrong, Watson traveled to London to meet Wilkins. While there, Wilkins showed Watson some new X-ray diffraction images created by Franklin. Watson looked at the images carefully and suddenly could see how the DNA structure worked. On his return journey, he began to sketch out a new model based on two interconnected helical strands.

Watson's sketch looked like a ladder that twisted around itself. The rungs of the ladder were made up of pairs of base chemicals, each complementing the other. They, in turn, were connected to long strands of sugars and phosphates, which offered the "upright" supports of the ladder. Watson called this the "double helix."

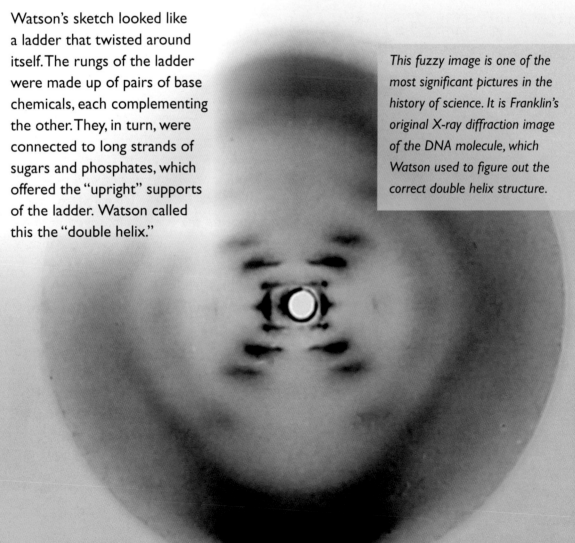

This fuzzy image is one of the most significant pictures in the history of science. It is Franklin's original X-ray diffraction image of the DNA molecule, which Watson used to figure out the correct double helix structure.

This is an illustration of the double helix structure of DNA. In the center are pairs of base chemicals, while the interwoven strands on the outside are sugars and phosphates.

BEHIND THE SCIENCE

Watson and Crick's double helix model explains how **DNA** carries the information needed to replicate cells and pass on genetic information. Each half of the double helix "ladder" forms a template for the other half. When cells divide to create new cells, the double helix ladder splits in half. Two new **DNA** molecules are then created from each half-ladder template.

The Secret of Life

When Watson returned to Cambridge, he showed his sketch to Crick. There was still work to do, but it looked like they may have solved science's greatest mystery. Crick certainly believed so. That night, he declared: "We've just discovered the secret of life!" Watson and Crick's model of the double helix was finished on March 7, 1953.

CHAPTER 5

The Discovery That Changed the World

On April 25, 1953, the scientific journal *Nature* featured an article by Watson and Crick entitled *Molecular Structure of Nucleic Acids*. In it they explained their double helix model for the structure of DNA. Over the months and years to come, the double helix model was proven to be correct.

Watson and Crick were also right about the implications of the double helix model. Research confirmed that the double helix contained all 46 human chromosomes and therefore each of the thousands of genes that carry the information about the personality characteristics, appearance, and body functions of each human. DNA is found in all living things, so Watson and Crick's discovery had much wider implications than understanding the genetic coding of the human body. It meant that scientists understood how all life on Earth continues to exist.

In the 60 years since Watson and Crick's discovery, scientists have figured out that all living organisms, from jaguars to trees, are governed by the DNA stored deep within their cells.

Watson and Crick's discovery of the double helix structure of DNA is so significant that it continues to inspire artists to create fabulous DNA sculptures such as this one made of metal, glass, and plastic.

Winning the Nobel Prize

In 1962, Watson, Crick, and Wilkins were jointly awarded the Nobel Prize for Physics in honor of their DNA research. Franklin, whose X-ray diffraction images had made such a difference, did not live to see it. She died of cancer in 1958, just 37 years old. Had she been alive, she would almost certainly have received the same prize.

IN THEIR OWN WORDS

In their article published in *Nature*, Watson and Crick wrote:

"It has not escaped our notice that the model we have proposed immediately suggests a possible copying mechanism for the genetic material."

A New World of Discovery

In the years following Watson and Crick's discovery, scientists from around the world built on their work. In the process, scientists increased people's understanding of DNA and its functions. Through this increased understanding have come a number of scientific breakthroughs.

One of the most notable achievements took place in 1972 when researchers at the biochemistry department at Stanford University created DNA from scratch. They called this recombinant DNA, or R-DNA. In the years that followed, scientists and drug companies used their research to create "synthetic DNA" to help cure diseases and treat lifelong illnesses such as diabetes.

Diabetics must test their blood sugar levels several times each day. If it is low, they can inject themselves with synthetic insulin, created using R-DNA.

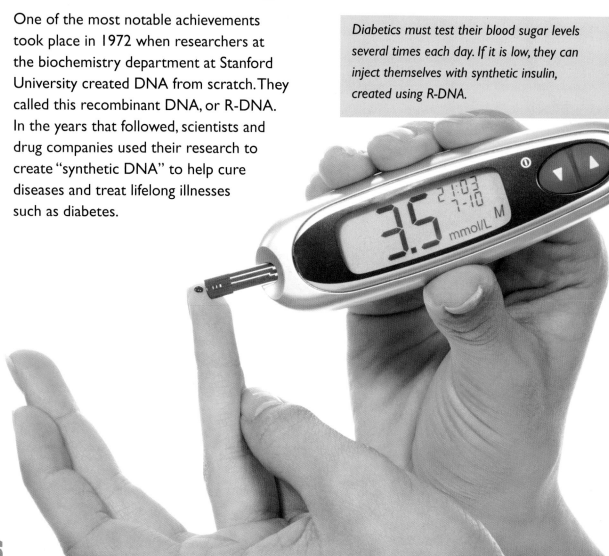

In the 1990s, scientists figured out that you could "clone" animals by making an exact copy of their DNA. The first animal created using this process, Dolly the Sheep, became a worldwide sensation and even appeared on stamps!

BEHIND THE SCIENCE

It is possible to create **R-DNA** because the chemical structure of DNA molecules across many different species is the same. The genetic matter contained within the molecules differs, which means that scientists can take genes from different species, such as pigs and humans, and combine them to create new strands of **R-DNA**.

Genetic Discoveries

Over the last 60 years, much DNA research has focused on genetics and the many thousands of genes hidden inside the chromosomes featured in the trillions of cells inside human bodies. Genes are made of DNA, and they are hugely important. Each gene has a specific purpose: some control traits, such as eye color, while others control people's blood type or their resistance to certain diseases.

37

Saving Lives and Convicting Criminals

As scientists continued to research **DNA** and genes, they realized that **DNA** contains instructions that tell our genes how to function. They discovered that every person's genes are unique so, as a result, everyone's **DNA** is different, too.

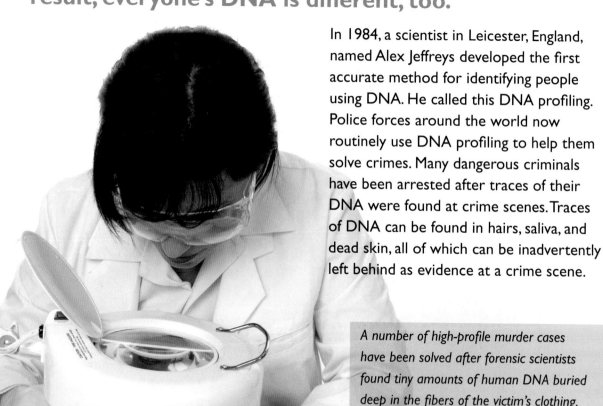

In 1984, a scientist in Leicester, England, named Alex Jeffreys developed the first accurate method for identifying people using DNA. He called this DNA profiling. Police forces around the world now routinely use DNA profiling to help them solve crimes. Many dangerous criminals have been arrested after traces of their DNA were found at crime scenes. Traces of DNA can be found in hairs, saliva, and dead skin, all of which can be inadvertently left behind as evidence at a crime scene.

A number of high-profile murder cases have been solved after forensic scientists found tiny amounts of human DNA buried deep in the fibers of the victim's clothing.

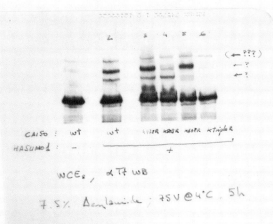
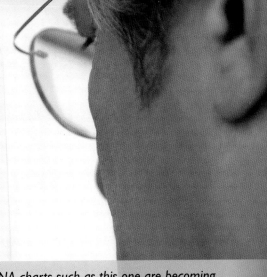

DNA charts such as this one are becoming increasingly common in hospitals as scientists and doctors look to gene therapy to cure dangerous hereditary diseases.

DNA in Medicine

In medicine, the use of R-DNA has become widespread. The first R-DNA created for medical use in humans was a form of artificial insulin. Insulin is found within our bodies and is needed to control the amount of sugar in our blood. Synthetic insulin was created using R-DNA in 1982 and is used to treat people with an insulin deficiency.

Another growing area is what scientists call gene therapy, which is the use of DNA to treat disease. Gene therapy was first used in 1990 and is a growing industry. It is commonly used to treat genetic diseases, which are illnesses passed from parents to their children.

BEHIND THE SCIENCE

In gene therapy, DNA is used to alter damaged genes. Sick patients with potentially life-threatening genetic diseases are treated with R-DNA. Inside the body, this R-DNA helps create healthy genes to replace damaged or mutated ones.

39

CHAPTER 6

A Lifetime Apart

Following their landmark discovery in Cambridge, Watson and Crick went their separate ways. They remained friends and occasional collaborators and in 1956 reunited to write a research paper on the molecular structure of small viruses. It was one of their last published papers together.

Crick continued to work in DNA research after parting company with Watson, and in 1958 he announced that he had solved the problem of how proteins are created within the body—a puzzle that had eluded even his great rival, Pauling. Crick continued to work in Cambridge and during the 1960s became fascinated with the origin of life, attempting to answer the question of how DNA developed in the first place. He could not find the answers he was looking for, and as his career progressed, his scientific interests changed. In 1976, Crick moved to southern California in order to work at the Salk Institute for Biological Studies.

Crick left Cambridge for the futuristic surroundings of California's Salk Institute after deciding to turn away from DNA research in favor of studying the human brain.

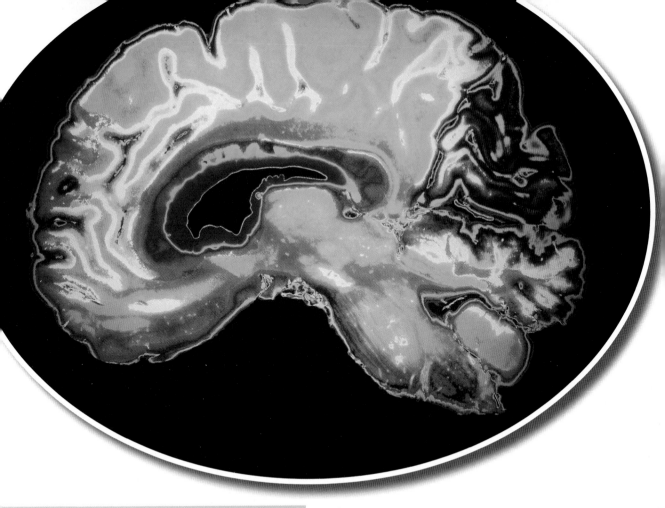

Crick was fascinated by how little people understand the brain, particularly about how it works when we are asleep. He spent the last 20 years of his career trying to discover more.

Investigating the Human Brain

Crick remained in California for the rest of his life, switching his focus to conduct research into the way the human brain works. Crick knew little about the way the brain works when he began his study of it, but he persevered with his studies and his knowledge grew. Crick continued working until his death in 2004. His great friend and partner, Watson, gave a moving speech at Crick's memorial service in San Jose, California.

IN THEIR OWN WORDS

The brain fascinated Crick. He said:

"There is no scientific study more vital to man than the study of his own brain. Our entire view of the universe depends on it."

41

The Next Great Discovery

In 1968, Watson left Cambridge and traveled back to the United States to take up a position at Harvard University. Before leaving Britain, he published *The Double Helix*, his account of the race to discover the structure of DNA.

The Double Helix caused much controversy, because Watson wrote as much about his personal experiences and his disputes with fellow scientists as he did about the science. Crick and Wilkins both objected to things Watson wrote about them.

The Human Genome is so long and complex that it fills more than 100 books, each 1,000 pages long—and is printed in type so small a person can barely read it! It can be found at the Wellcome Collection in London where it sits in a special bookcase.

Human Genome Project

Watson continued to work in genetics and in 1990 was appointed as the head of the Human Genome Project, a study featuring scientists in the United States and Britain. Over 11 years, scientists painstakingly studied and noted down every single gene in the human body. In 2001, the first draft of the Human Genome Project was completed. It revealed every single gene in the human body and its function. The team discovered that each human has more than 21,000 different genes.

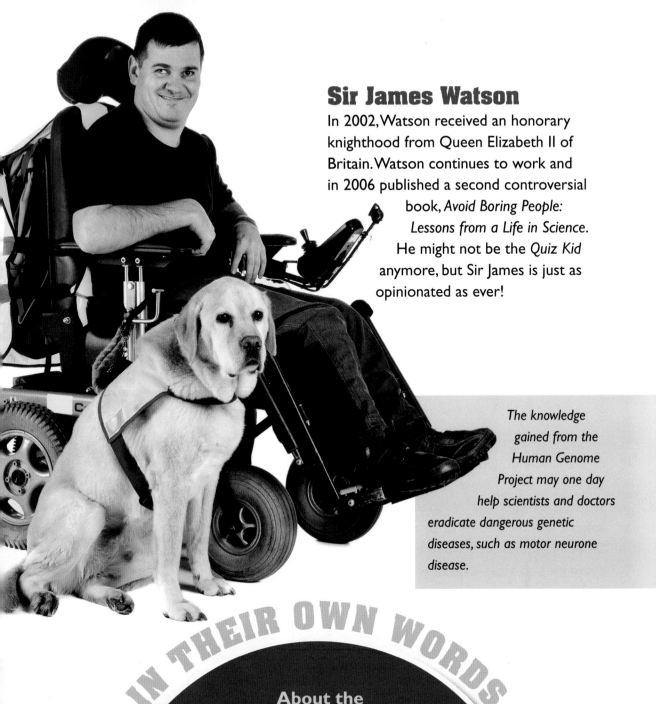

Sir James Watson

In 2002, Watson received an honorary knighthood from Queen Elizabeth II of Britain. Watson continues to work and in 2006 published a second controversial book, *Avoid Boring People: Lessons from a Life in Science.* He might not be the *Quiz Kid* anymore, but Sir James is just as opinionated as ever!

The knowledge gained from the Human Genome Project may one day help scientists and doctors eradicate dangerous genetic diseases, such as motor neurone disease.

IN THEIR OWN WORDS

About the
Human Genome Project,
Watson said:

"Not all our genes are perfect, and often these imperfections lead to quite serious diseases . . . the imperfections seemed as important as the perfections."

Dynamic Differences

Few scientists have changed the world around us quite like Watson and Crick. Their story is a remarkable one. The two scientists worked together for just over two years but, in that time, made one of the most dramatic and dynamic discoveries in the history of science. They were very different people, but both were opinionated, loved to talk, and frequently argued. When they were working together, their arguments seemed to spur them on to even greater achievements.

When Watson and Crick first proposed their model of the double helix, it barely made the pages of the local newspaper in Cambridge. Yet, within a few months, the scientists had become famous around the world. By explaining how DNA molecules are structured, the scientists set in motion a chain of events that has changed science forever.

Crick and Watson's discovery changed the world, but it also made them famous across the globe. The double helix model is now one of the most recognizable scientific images around the world.

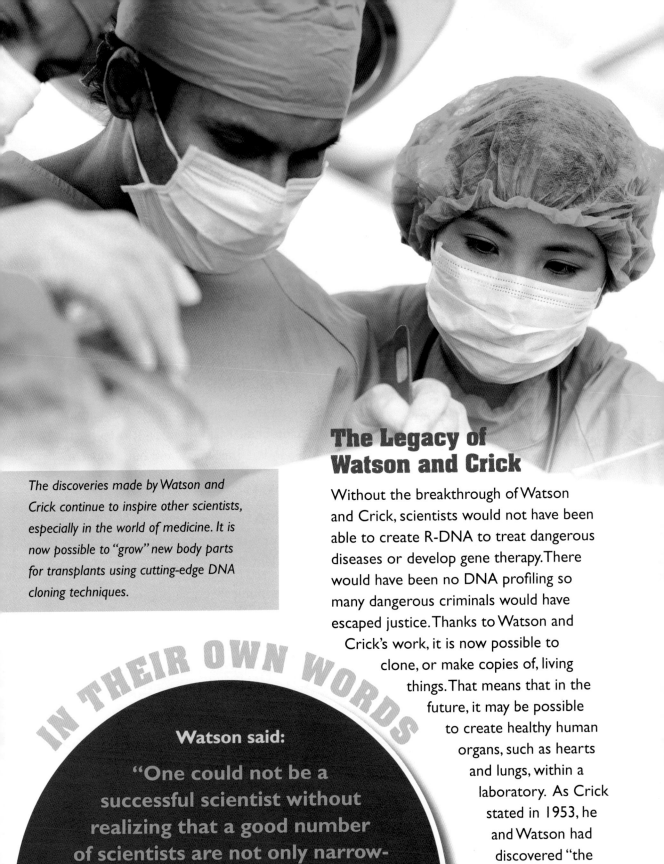

The discoveries made by Watson and Crick continue to inspire other scientists, especially in the world of medicine. It is now possible to "grow" new body parts for transplants using cutting-edge DNA cloning techniques.

The Legacy of Watson and Crick

Without the breakthrough of Watson and Crick, scientists would not have been able to create R-DNA to treat dangerous diseases or develop gene therapy. There would have been no DNA profiling so many dangerous criminals would have escaped justice. Thanks to Watson and Crick's work, it is now possible to clone, or make copies of, living things. That means that in the future, it may be possible to create healthy human organs, such as hearts and lungs, within a laboratory. As Crick stated in 1953, he and Watson had discovered "the secret of life."

IN THEIR OWN WORDS

Watson said:

"One could not be a successful scientist without realizing that a good number of scientists are not only narrow-minded and dull, but also just stupid."

Glossary

alpha helix the shape of a protein molecule, so called because it is helical in shape. This means it looks a little like a coiled spring

amino acid a type of acid that occurs naturally in the body. Our bodies require amino acids to build protein

cells the building blocks of life. All living things, including humans, are made up of billions of tiny individual cells

chromosome the part of the cell that contains the genes

DNA (deoxyribonucleic acid) an extremely long, but very small, molecule that is the main component of chromosomes

DNA profiling the process of studying someone's DNA in order to identify them

double helix the name given to the shape of the DNA molecule by Watson and Crick, so called because it looks like two coiled springs (or helixes) wrapped around each other

enrolled signed up for

gene a part of a cell, located on a chromosome, that controls appearance, growth, and other traits of a living thing

genetics the study of human genes and how people pass on traits to their children

goniometer a machine used for studying the structure of molecules

microscope a device used for looking at very small objects

molecular biology the study of cells, molecules, and atoms in the natural world (including humans)

molecule two or more atoms joined together

photographic paper the paper used to print photographs

proteins molecules made from amino acids. Their main function it is to heal wounds, fight illness, and build muscle

replicate to reproduce

R-DNA (recombinant DNA) a form of DNA created from scratch in a laboratory by scientists

virus a microscopic organism that grows and multiplies inside the body

X-ray crystallographer a scientist who specializes in using X-ray diffraction techniques to study the structure of molecules

X-ray diffraction the process of firing invisible X-rays at a molecule in order to create an image of the molecule on photographic paper

X-rays waves of energy that are invisible to the human eye but can be seen with the aid of special equipment

For More Information

Books

Rand, Casey. *DNA and Heredity* (Investigating Cells). Portsmouth, NH: Heinemann, 2010.

Schafer, Susan. *DNA and Genes* (Genetics: The Science of Life). Armonk, NY: M.E. Sharpe, 2009.

Stille, Darlene R., and Eric Hoffman. *DNA: The Master Molecule of Life* (Exploring Science). North Mankato, MN: Compass Point Books, 2006.

Websites

For an easy-to-understand introduction to genes and DNA, log on to Kids Health at:
kidshealth.org/kid/talk/qa/what_is_gene.html

Find out more about genetics at:
www.chem4kids.com/files/bio_dna.html

Have you ever wondered how and why you have the same color eyes as your mom or dad? This easy-to-follow guide explains all at:
www.sciencekidsathome.com/science_topics/genetics-a.html

Publisher's note to educators and parents: Our editors have carefully reviewed these websites to ensure that they are suitable for students. Many websites change frequently, however, and we cannot guarantee that a site's future contents will continue to meet our high standards of quality and educational value. Be advised that students should be closely supervised whenever they access the Internet.

Index